NATURE CLOSE-UP

BUTTERFLIES and MOTHS

TEXT BY ELAINE PASCOE

PHOTOGRAPHS BY DWIGHT KUHN

BLACKBIRCH PRESS, INC.

WOODBRIDGE, CONNECTICUT

Published by Blackbirch Press, Inc.
260 Amity Road
Woodbridge, CT 06525

©1997 by Blackbirch Press, Inc.
Text ©1997 by Elaine Pascoe
Photographs ©1997 by Dwight Kuhn
First Edition

Printed in the United States
10 9 8 7 6 5 4 3 2 1

front cover: painted lady butterfly
back cover: (left to right) monarch caterpillar, monarch caterpillar molting to form chrysalis, monarch chrysalis, monarch butterfly

Library of Congress Cataloging-in-Publication Data
Pascoe, Elaine.
Butterflies and Moths / by Elaine Pascoe. — 1st ed.
      p.   cm. — (Nature close up)
    Includes bibliographical references (p.) and index.
    Summary: Investigates the physical characteristics, reproductive processes, habitats, and metamorphoses of butterflies and moths through hands-on projects.
    ISBN 1-56711-180-7 (alk. paper)
    1. Butterflies—Juvenile literature. 2. Moths—Juvenile literature. 3. Butterflies—Experiments—Juvenile literature. 4. Moths—Experiments—Juvenile literature. 5. Butterflies as pets—Juvenile literature. 6. Moths as pets—Juvenile literature. [1. Butterflies. 2. Moths. 3. Butterflies—Experiments. 4. Moths—Experiments. 5. Experiments.] I. Title. II. Series: Pascoe, Elaine. Nature Close-Up
QL544.2.P35   1997   95-42704
595.78—dc20   CIP
                                                          AC

Note on metric conversions: The metric conversions given in Chapters 2 and 3 of this book are not always exact equivalents of U.S. measures. Instead, they provide a workable quantity for each experiment in metric units. The abbreviations used are:

cm	centimeter	**g**	gram
m	meter	**kg**	kilogram
km	kilometer	**l**	liter

CONTENTS

1

Flying Flowers

Butterflies and moths include some of the most beautiful insects in the world. When these colorful creatures flutter over a garden, they look like flowers that have let go of their stems and taken to the air.

Butterflies and moths have a fascinating life cycle as well. They hatch from eggs as leaf-eating caterpillars that can't fly at all. Then, through a bit of natural magic called metamorphosis, they change into winged adults that feed on flower nectar. Most adult butterflies and moths have little in common with their caterpillars. It's hard to believe they are actually the same insect at two different stages of life—but that is what they are!

These remarkable insects live all over the world, except in cold polar regions. There are thousands of kinds, or species—more than 7,000 in North America alone. They range from tiny creatures such as the American nepticulid, or midget moth, with a wingspread of about an eighth of an inch (.32 cm), to insects that are bigger than some birds. Some of the largest species live in Australia and New Guinea. They include the giant Hercules moth, which has a wingspan of 10 inches (25.4 cm), and the Queen Alexandra birdwing butterfly, with a wingspan of 11 inches (27.9 cm).

Opposite: **Monarch butterfly**

SCALY WINGS

Butterflies and moths all belong to the same insect family. The scientific name for this family, Lepidoptera, means "scaly winged" in Greek. The wings of butterflies and moths are covered with thousands of tiny overlapping scales.

If you've ever touched the wing of a butterfly or moth, you've probably found that a fine powder came off on your fingers. The "powder" is made up of scales from the wing—they fall off at the slightest touch. This is a great advantage to a butterfly or moth that blunders into a spider's web. A few of its scales may stick to the web, but the insect will probably escape unharmed.

Above: **An electron-microscope view of a butterfly wing shows the individual scales.**
Right: **A magnifying-lens view of a butterfly wing shows many scales. The scales give the wings their patterns and colors.**

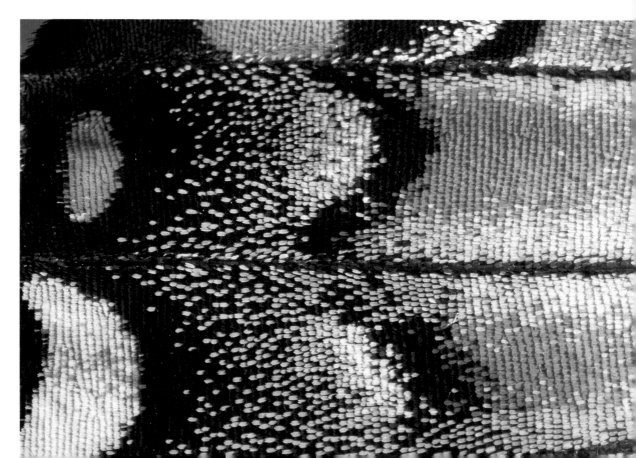

Many moths have colors and patterns that help them to blend in with their surroundings. This protects them from predators.

The scales give the wings their patterns and colors and, in many cases, a sparkly, iridescent sheen. Many butterflies and some moths sport bright hues and bold designs on their wings. The colors and designs help them identify others of their species and, thus, find mates. Others, especially moths, are mottled shades of brown and tan. This camouflages them; that is, the coloring helps them blend in with their surroundings, and, thus, escape birds and other predators that would like to eat them. And some butterflies have it both ways. Their wings are boldly patterned on top, so that they flash with color when the insect flies. But when the butterfly rests, only the undersides of its wings show, and they are dull and drab.

A BUTTERFLY MIMIC

The viceroy butterfly has a clever disguise. This beautiful orange-and-black insect looks just like a monarch butterfly. Birds and other predators avoid monarchs because they taste awful. Since predators can't tell a viceroy from a monarch, they avoid the viceroy, too.

Viceroy (left); monarch (right)

The wings of painted lady butterflies are drab when they are closed (top left) but brightly colored when open (bottom left).

A great spangled fritillary butterfly drinks nectar from a black-eyed susan.

FLIERS

Like all insects, butter-flies and moths have six legs and a hard shell, or exoskeleton, rather than a bony internal skeleton. They have so many other features in common that it's often hard to know whether you're looking at a butterfly or a moth. Here are a few differences to look for—but remember that there are exceptions to all these guidelines:

- Butterflies are usually active during the day, while moths tend to be active at night.
- Many butterflies are more brightly colored than moths.
- Butterflies usually hold their wings up when they rest; moths fold their wings down.

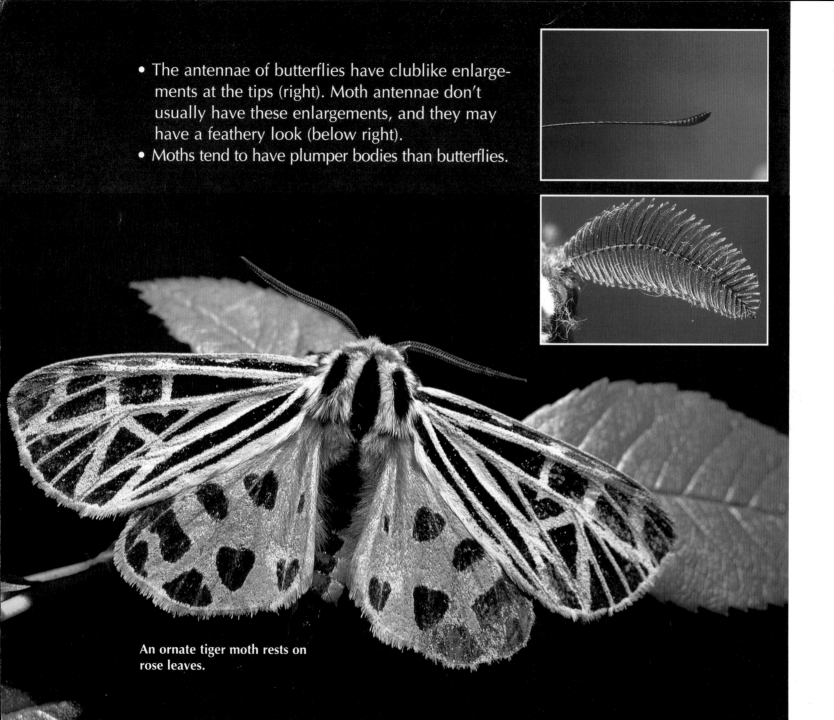

- The antennae of butterflies have clublike enlargements at the tips (right). Moth antennae don't usually have these enlargements, and they may have a feathery look (below right).
- Moths tend to have plumper bodies than butterflies.

An ornate tiger moth rests on rose leaves.

Most butterflies and many moths feed on the sugary nectar of flowers. When the insect finds a flower it likes, it unrolls its proboscis, a long tube that can suck nectar and other liquids into its mouth. Butterflies taste with their feet, so they know as soon as they land on a flower whether it will give them a good meal or not. Moths have taste organs called palpi just below the head.

Tiger swallowtails, like all butterflies, actually taste with their feet.

Above: **A flower has a different appearance in ultraviolet light (left) and normal light (right).**
Left: **The large antennae of this male luna moth help it find a female of its species so that they can mate.**

Butterflies and moths also find flowers by sight. They are sensitive to ultraviolet light, which people are not able to see. To them, flowers seem to glow with colors we can't detect. And these insects can smell flowers with their sensitive antennae. The antennae of males have another important purpose: to help the insect find a female of its species, so that they can mate. The male detects the scent of chemicals produced by the female and flies to her.

LEAF EATERS

After mating, a female butterfly or moth lays anywhere from 50 to 1,000 eggs. Only some of these will hatch, and of those that do, only a few will survive to become adult butterflies or moths. Most of the rest will be eaten by predators at some point in their lives.

The female places the eggs on plants that will provide food for the young caterpillars when they hatch. Many caterpillars will eat only certain kinds of leaves. Monarch caterpillars, for example, eat only milkweed leaves. (They absorb a toxic substance from the milkweed, which doesn't harm them but makes both the caterpillars and the adults taste terrible to predators.) So female monarch butterflies carefully lay their eggs on milkweed plants. A few types of moth caterpillars eat foods other than plants. Clothes moths, for example, lay their eggs on wool and silk fabrics. Their caterpillars eat these fibers—and can ruin clothing that's not properly stored for protection.

A monarch butterfly laid this egg on a milkweed plant so that its caterpillar would have a handy food supply when it hatched.

Caterpillars, like this monarch caterpillar, begin to eat as soon as they hatch.

Young caterpillars may hatch in a week or so, or the eggs may be dormant (inactive) for months. When the caterpillars come out, they are tiny—and hungry. They start right away to eat, chewing up leaves or plant fibers with their strong jaws. A caterpillar does little besides eat and grow. As it gets bigger, its skin becomes tight. Finally, the skin splits open, and the caterpillar wriggles out of its old skin, ready to continue growing in a new skin. This process occurs several times as the caterpillar grows.

Caterpillars are a favorite meal for birds and other predators. Many caterpillars are well camouflaged; others have bold patterns that confuse predators. Many caterpillars spin silken thread from a gland near their mouth. The thread helps give them a foothold as they inch along over leaves and branches, gripping tightly with their little clawed feet. If a caterpillar is touched or threatened, it may let go of its branch and drop to the ground on a silken lifeline, much as a startled spider will do. A caterpillar has six eyes on each side of its head, just above its mouth. But these see little more than light and dark—mostly, the caterpillar feels its way with its antennae.

14

BECOMING AN ADULT

After weeks, sometimes months, of eating and growing, a caterpillar is ready to pupate, entering the next stage in its life cycle. A butterfly caterpillar spins a button of silk that will hold it firmly to a sturdy stem or leaf. It sheds its skin once again (photo 1) and emerges as a pupa, or chrysalis, surrounded by a hard shell (photo 2). Inside, the pupa begins to change into an adult butterfly. Sometimes this change takes only a couple of weeks, but many types of butterflies stay in the pupa stage longer. Some do not emerge as butterflies until the next spring.

Near the end of this time, the chrysalis shell may become so thin that you can see the new butterfly's wings inside (photo 3). Finally, it splits, and the new butterfly wriggles out. At first, its wings are limp, damp, and crumpled. They unfold as blood flows into them, and they stiffen as they dry (photo 4). Then the butterfly can fly.

1.

Pupating stages of the butterfly (monarch shown here)

2.

3.

4.

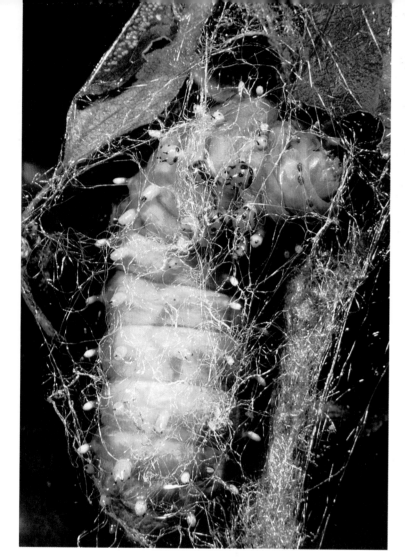

Moth caterpillars change into adults in much the same way that butterflies do. Many kinds of moth caterpillars spin a silken cocoon (see photos above, which show a cecropia moth) that will help protect them as pupae. Only a few types of butterflies spin cocoons.

WORLD TRAVELERS

Migration is the seasonal travel, or movement, of animals. Some butterflies migrate over amazing distances. Painted ladies, which are found in many parts of the world, fly between California and Hawaii and between Iceland and North Africa. Monarchs travel 2,000 miles (3,218.6 km) from the eastern United States and Canada to winter in Mexico. They fly north again in spring, mating along the way and laying eggs that will hatch to create the next generation of monarchs. Migrating butterflies take advantage of air currents high in the atmosphere—they float, rather than fly, for much of the way. Flocks of migrating butterflies have been spotted at altitudes of 7,000 feet (2,133.6 m).

Many types of butterflies and moths live for just a few weeks in summer. A few kinds hibernate through winter, resting under piles of leaves or in other sheltered spots. And some gather in flocks of millions and head south when the weather turns cool. But none live more than 18 months. Their goal during this short time is to find a mate and reproduce, beginning the cycle of life again.

BUTTERFLIES, MOTHS, AND PEOPLE

While many people are happy to see butterflies and moths, not so many feel the same way about caterpillars. Hungry caterpillars can do a great deal of damage to crops and gardens, so farmers and gardeners often kill them with pesticides. Still, butterflies and moths usually lay enough eggs to ensure that some will survive.

Some types of butterflies and moths are becoming scarcer, however, and pesticides are not the only danger that they face. Many of these insects lay their eggs on only a few types of plants. As people develop land for farming, housing, and other uses, the habitats of butterflies and moths are destroyed. Plants that the butterflies and moths depend on are harder to find. That makes it more difficult for the insects to survive.

Caterpillars look very different from the butterflies and moths they become. *Clockwise from top left:* black swallowtail butterfly; black swallowtail caterpillar; painted lady caterpillar; painted lady butterfly.

Clockwise from top left: cecropia moth; cecropia moth caterpillar; luna moth caterpillar; luna moth.

Butterflies and moths hold an important place in the web of life. As they fly from flower to flower, sipping nectar, they help pollinate plants, so that plants can reproduce. And as adults and caterpillars, these insects are an important source of food for birds and other animals. In this way, they are much more than a pretty sight.

19

2

Keeping Butterflies, Moths, and Their Caterpillars

Butterflies and moths usually flash past so quickly that it's difficult to get more than a brief glimpse of them. Caterpillars can be hard to spot at all—most blend in with their surroundings. But you can learn a great deal about these insects, as adults or caterpillars, by keeping them at home and observing them for a short time. If you can provide them with the food and living conditions they need, observing and learning about them isn't hard to do. You may even be able to raise a moth or butterfly from caterpillar to adult, watching it change before your eyes.

You can collect caterpillars, pupae, and adult butterflies and moths in the wild, or you can buy caterpillars, cocoons, or chrysalises from a biological supply house. (See the sources on page 46.) Remember that the numbers of many kinds of these insects are declining. Collect only a few caterpillars or adults, and care for them well. When you have finished observing the insects, release them. Be sure to release them in the place where you found them or in a place where the same types of plants are growing.

Spring and summer are the best times to look for caterpillars and butterflies. This boy examines a cabbage butterfly resting on a zinnia.

21

COLLECTING CATERPILLARS, EGGS, AND PUPAE

Look for caterpillars in spring and summer, on branches, stems, and leaves of plants. Take along a small container. Ask an adult to help you punch small holes in the top so that air can get in. Or make a top out of a piece of nylon mesh (such as a piece cut from an old pair of pantyhose or an old sheer curtain) secured with a rubber band.

When you find a caterpillar, put it in your container along with some stems and leaves of the plant on which you found it. Some caterpillars with spines or hairs can irritate the skin if touched. Rather than picking up the caterpillar, break off the leaf or stem that the caterpillar is on and place it—caterpillar and all—in your container.

Note the kind of plant that the caterpillar is on. It is probably a food plant for the insect, and you will need to provide more of its leaves as the caterpillar grows. Don't leave the container in direct sunlight; it will quickly grow too hot for the caterpillars.

You may find butterfly or moth eggs attached to the stems or leaves of certain plants, such as milkweed. If you collect eggs, take them along with the leaves that they are attached to—don't separate them from the leaves. Put the eggs and leaves in a caterpillar home (see pages 23–24). Keep the soil in the home moist, and keep a supply of fresh leaves of the same type of plant in the container with the eggs. When the caterpillars hatch, they will need food to eat.

Later in the year, you may find a moth cocoon or a butterfly chrysalis attached to a twig. These are hard to spot, so you will have to look carefully. Don't try to separate the cocoon or chrysalis from the plant. Instead, break off the twig and put it in your container. See the instructions for caring for pupae on page 25.

The hairs on some caterpillars, such as this gypsy moth caterpillar, can irritate your skin if you touch them.

CARING FOR CATERPILLARS

Move your caterpillars from their collection container to a more permanent home as soon as possible. A large jar will be fine. Put some moist soil and a few dried leaves in the bottom, and keep the soil moist by lightly misting it with water. This will keep the moisture level in the container high. The soil and leaves may serve another purpose: Some caterpillars make cocoons in these materials.

Place your caterpillars in the jar along with fresh stems or twigs and leaves from the plants on which you found them. Lightly sprinkle some water on the leaves. Cover the top of the container with mesh, secured by a rubber band. Keep the container out of direct sunlight.

A large jar makes a good caterpillar home.

23

You can also use an old fish tank as a caterpillar home. Add moist soil and leaves as above. Cut a piece of mesh big enough to cover the top with an inch (a couple of centimeters) or more to spare on all sides. Tape the mesh to the tank three fourths of the way around, using electrical tape, duct tape, or other strong tape. Leave a loose flap at one end so that you can reach into the container to clean it or add leaves. At other times, the flap can be taped down temporarily to prevent the caterpillars from escaping.

Add fresh stems and leaves when the caterpillars have eaten most of their supply or when the greenery in the container begins to wilt. Large caterpillars eat a lot—you may have to give them fresh leaves daily. Leaves will stay fresh longer if you place the stems in a small container of water. To keep the caterpillars from moving down the stem and falling in the water, stuff cotton balls around the top of the water container.

Caterpillars make a lot of waste, especially as they grow bigger. Clean the container and replace the soil when you see wastes building up.

CARING FOR PUPAE

When your caterpillars grow large, they will need a place to pupate. A large container, such as one of the butterfly houses described on the following pages, is best for this. Some caterpillars pupate among the leaves of their food plants. Some move down to soil or leaf litter. And some crawl off to other places. If you don't know what your caterpillars will do, provide everything they may need—moist soil, dried leaves, food plants, and sturdy twigs that they can crawl on.

Some butterflies and moths have a short pupa stage. You will see adults emerge in a few weeks. Others stay in the pupa stage through winter and don't come out until spring. If adults haven't emerged when cold weather begins, put the container in a cold place, such as an unheated garage or even outdoors. If you keep the container indoors, adults may develop too quickly and emerge before the weather is warm enough for them to survive outdoors.

When the weather begins to warm up in spring, check the container each day, and sprinkle it lightly with water. When leaves and flowers appear outside, you can safely bring the container indoors for closer observation, if you want. Be sure the container is large enough for the adults to unfold and dry their wings. Release the adults as they emerge.

COLLECTING BUTTERFLIES AND MOTHS

Look for butterflies around gardens and near wildflowers in summer. To find moths, turn on a porch light or another outdoor light. These night fliers are drawn to light, and they will probably come to you—along with a lot of other insects!

To collect adult butterflies and moths, you will need a net. You can buy a butterfly net from sources such as those on page 46, but it's easy to make one.

What to Do:

1. Bend the clothes hanger to form a round loop. Straighten the hanger's hook. (Ask an adult to help if the hanger is hard to bend.)
2. If you're using piece of fabric or a section of material cut from an old curtain, fold the material in half and sew two of the three open edges closed, to form a deep pouch.
3. Put your pouch or mesh laundry bag through the wire loop. At the open end, fold the fabric over the wire loop, and sew it in place.
4. Tape the net to the handle.

Use the net in a gentle sweeping action to catch a butterfly or moth. When you have caught one, carry it home in the net, and place the insect in a butterfly house (see pages 28–29). Be careful not to handle the delicate wings, which can be easily damaged. Touch only the body of the insect.

If the insect was feeding when you caught it, note the type of flower you found it on, and collect some of the blossoms.

What You Need:
* A mop or broom handle
* Duct tape or black electrical tape
* A piece of fine mesh fabric, a large mesh laundry bag, or a section from an old sheer curtain
* A wire clothes hanger
* Needle and thread

CARING FOR BUTTERFLIES AND MOTHS

It's best to prepare a home for the butterflies and moths before you collect them. These insects are happiest with a lot of flying space and will not live long in small containers. Keep butterflies and moths only as long as you need to observe them, at most a day or two. They will live and mate better in the wild.

You can keep butterflies and moths in a screen cage. To make one, buy a section of wire screening at a hardware store. Roll it into a tube, fastening it with staples at the top and bottom or by tying string around it. Use cake tins to make the top and bottom of the cage. Or make a larger tube, setting it directly on newspaper and using a trash-can lid or other large cover for the top.

Butterflies and moths need a fairly large home.

A tent with mesh windows can be used as a home for butterflies and moths.

You can also make a butterfly house from a large cardboard carton, at least a couple of feet on each side. Ask an adult to help you cut big "windows" in all four sides of the carton. Cover these with screening or netting, taping or stapling it in place. The top can be temporarily taped shut after you place the insects inside. If you have a small camping tent and a place in your yard to pitch it, you can use that as a butterfly home, too.

Butterflies feed on flower nectar. Some moths don't feed at all, but it's best to provide food anyway, in case you've collected a type that needs it. Place a bouquet of fresh flowers in a container of water in the cage. Include kinds that were blooming where you found the insect.

Left: It's best if you can provide fresh flowers for your butterflies, which normally eat nectar.
Right: If flowers aren't available, however, you can feed your butterflies sugar water.

If you can't provide fresh flowers, you can feed butterflies and moths with a mixture of sugar or honey and water. Mix one part sugar or honey with nine parts water (one spoonful of sugar in nine spoonfuls of water, for example). Put this in a small, shallow container with some cotton balls or a piece of clean sponge. Put in enough solution to just reach the top of the cotton balls or sponge. Make a landing place for the butterflies by draping a small piece of mesh or gauze over the side of the container.

3

Investigating Butterflies and Moths

Butterflies and moths are fascinating to watch, and so are their caterpillars. On the following pages, you'll find some activities that will help you learn more about these small animals. Try to disturb the insects as little as possible when you do these activities, and be careful not to touch the wings of butterflies and moths.

Remember to keep adult butterflies and moths for just a short time, a day or so at most. Then release them, so that they can complete their life cycle. If you can't provide caterpillars with the conditions they need to pupate—or don't want to keep them through that stage—release them where you found them or on the same type of plant, to let them grow into adults.

Opposite: **A viceroy caterpillar crawls along a leaf.**

33

What You Need:

* Several caterpillars of the same type
* Butterfly house or caterpillar home
* Stems and leaves of various green plants
* Container for water and plant material
* Adhesive labels or masking tape for making labels
* Cotton balls

Lilac

WHAT DO CATERPILLARS LIKE TO EAT?

In the wild, you will almost always find caterpillars crawling on plants and eating leaves. That is practically all they do. You can guess that they eat the leaves of the plants on which you find them. Will they eat other types of leaves as well? Here's a way to find out.

What to Do:

1. Collect several caterpillars of the same kind, along with stems and leaves of the plants on which you found them. Collect stems and leaves of several other kinds of plants as well.

2. Try to identify the plants you've collected. Your library may have plant guides that will help. Label the plants, folding an adhesive label or a strip of masking tape around each stem. (If you can't identify the plants, you can label them with letters or numbers.)

3. Place the plant stems in a container of water. Wedge cotton balls into the container opening to keep the stems in place. This will also prevent the caterpillars from crawling down the stems and falling into the water, where they might drown.

4. Put the container in the butterfly house or caterpillar home, and place caterpillars on the various kinds of plants. (A butterfly house works best for this activity; it provides more space for the plants than a small caterpillar container.)

5. Watch the caterpillars for several days. Replace the plant stems when the leaves wilt or are eaten, putting in a fresh stem of the same type of plant.

Results: Note which plants the caterpillars eat. Keep a record of your findings.
Conclusion: What do your results tell you about your caterpillars' food preferences? If you like, you can repeat this experiment with different kinds of plants—or with different kinds of caterpillars. (Be sure that your container always includes leaves of the type of plant on which you found the caterpillars.)

DO CATERPILLARS GROW FASTER IN WARM OR COOL TEMPERATURES?

In cold-winter climates, caterpillars do not hatch until warm weather comes in spring. But even in spring, temperatures can be quite cool. Does temperature affect the way that caterpillars grow? Decide what you think, and then do this activity to see if you are right.

What to Do:

1. Place an equal number of caterpillars in each of the containers, along with an equal amount of stems and leaves from the plants on which they were found.
2. Keep one container indoors in a warm room (make sure it is not in direct sunlight; it will get too hot). Put the other in a cooler room or cool basement. Record the temperature in each place.
3. Try to keep conditions other than temperature the same in both containers. Make sure that the caterpillars in both containers always have plenty of fresh leaves to feed on—older caterpillars can grow fast and eat lots of leaves.
4. Every few days, measure the length of each caterpillar and record your findings.

Results: Do caterpillars grow more quickly in one location or the other?
Conclusion: What do your results tell you about the way temperature affects caterpillars? Do you think that caterpillars that hatch in early spring grow as quickly as those that hatch later in the year?

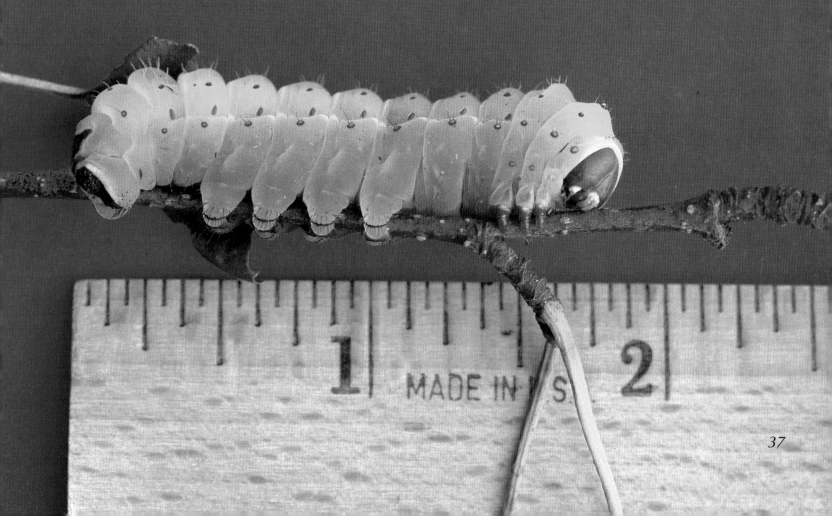

DO BUTTERFLIES PREFER SUGAR WATER OR FLOWER NECTAR?

Many butterflies and a few moths feed on flower nectar, which is naturally sweet. You can also offer them water that has been sweetened with sugar or honey. Which food do you think butterflies prefer? Make a prediction, and then do this to find out.

What to Do:
1. Place the butterflies in the butterfly house.
2. Fill one soda bottle with plain water, and put the flowers in it.
3. Cut away the top part of the paper cup, leaving a shallow bowl. Lay the gauze or screening in the bowl so that it hangs over the edges. Cut a piece of sponge to fit inside the bowl, and press it in on top of the gauze or screening.
4. Make a solution of sugar or honey and water, mixing one part sugar or honey to nine parts water. Mix it well, and let the sugar dissolve completely. Add some of this solution to the cup, so that it just covers the sponge.

38

What You Need:
* At least one butterfly
* Butterfly house
* Flowers
* Sugar or honey and water
* Two empty soda bottles, both the same size
* Paper cup
* Clean sponge, the same color as the flowers
* Scissors
* Small piece of gauze or screening

5. Put the bottle with the flowers in the butterfly house. Place the second soda bottle in the butterfly house, and set the cup with the sugar solution on top of it, so that it will be at the same height as the flowers.

6. Watch the butterflies to see where they feed.

Results: Check the butterfly house often. Where do you see the butterflies feeding? Make a record of your findings.

Conclusion: Was your prediction correct? How could you best attract butterflies—by growing flowers or by setting out a "butterfly feeder" filled with sugar water? Try this activity again, using different types of flowers. Use a sponge that is the same color as the flowers you choose.

DO BUTTERFLIES PREFER CERTAIN COLORS OR KINDS OF FLOWERS?

In a garden, butterflies move from flower to flower. Why do they land on some and skip others? This activity will help you find out.

What to Do:
1. Put the butterflies in the butterfly house.
2. Cut the stems of the flowers to equal lengths. Fill the container with water, and place the flowers in it. Separate the blossoms, so that a butterfly can easily land on any flower. If necessary, stuff cotton balls between the stems or place different colors of flowers in separate containers to keep them from being bunched tightly together.

What You Need:
* At least one butterfly
* Butterfly house
* Flowers of various colors
* Water container (or several containers) for the flowers
* Cotton balls (optional)

A great spangled fritillary butterfly uses its proboscis to suck nectar from a flower.

3. Put the flowers in the butterfly house, and watch the butterflies to see where they feed.

Results: Check the butterfly house often. Where do you see the butterflies feeding? Make a record of your findings.

Conclusion: Do the butterflies seem to prefer one color over another? You can repeat this experiment using flowers that are all the same color but different types or shapes.

MORE ACTIVITIES WITH BUTTERFLIES AND MOTHS

1. Take a close-up look at a caterpillar. How many feet does it have? How does it use its feet—do all the feet serve the same purpose? Watch the caterpillar eat. Does it finish eating one leaf completely before moving on to another?

2. Collect some caterpillars, set up a caterpillar home for them (see chapter 2), and keep a notebook recording how they grow and change. Measure them once a week and record their growth. Note how much they eat and how often they shed their skin. How does a caterpillar wriggle out of its old skin? (If you don't actually see the caterpillars shed, look for old skin attached to leaves.) Do the caterpillars change in color or appearance before they pupate? Illustrate your notebook with drawings of the caterpillars at various stages.

Above: A luna moth caterpillar holds onto a twig with its feet. *Right:* This monarch caterpillar is shedding its skin, just as all caterpillars do.

An adult cecropia moth emerges from its cocoon.

3. Collect a cocoon or chrysalis, or keep a caterpillar through the pupa stage, and watch as the adult emerges. This usually happens in mid- to late morning or early afternoon. You can often see that an adult butterfly is getting ready to emerge because the chrysalis becomes nearly transparent. How long does it take the adult to get out of its chrysalis or cocoon? How do the wings unfold? How long does it take the adult to fly away? Be sure to release the adult near the place where you originally found the caterpillar or pupa.

When you look closely, you can compare the different features of a butterfly (*left*—a crescentspot) and a moth (*right*—a cecropia).

4. Collect an adult butterfly and an adult moth, or several adults of different types. How are they different? How are they alike? Compare their physical features—their wings, bodies, antennae, and the like. Compare their behavior. When are they active? When do they feed? How do they hold their wings at rest? Can you identify the species (types) you have collected? Your library may have an insect guide that will help. Release the insects when you have finished your observations.

5. Watch butterflies in a field or garden that has many types of flowers. What flowers seem to attract them? Do they seem to prefer certain colors?

6. Plant a garden to attract butterflies to your home. A sunny corner, or even a window box, is all the space you need. Include a variety of flowers. Black-eyed susans, clover, coreopsis, daisies, marigolds, phlox, verbena, and zinnias are all good choices. Or plant a mix of wildflower seeds.

RESULTS AND CONCLUSIONS

Here are some possible results and conclusions for the activities on pages 34 to 41. Many factors may affect the outcomes of these activities—the types of insects you collect, the food you provide for them, and other conditions. If your results differ, try to think of some reasons why this might be so. Repeat the activity with different conditions, and see if your results are the same.

What Do Caterpillars Like to Eat?

Some caterpillars will eat the leaves of just one or two kinds of plants. Others aren't so picky. Gypsy moth caterpillars, for example, will devour the leaves of many kinds of trees and will even eat pine needles. Your results will depend on the type of caterpillar you have collected.

Do Caterpillars Grow Faster in Warm or Cool Temperatures?

Caterpillars generally grow more quickly in warm conditions. You may also find that the caterpillars kept in a warm room are more active and eat more leaves than the caterpillars kept in a cool place.

Do Butterflies Prefer Sugar Water or Flower Nectar?

Butterflies usually prefer flower nectar, but they will feed on sugar or honey solution when they can't get nectar.

Do Butterflies Prefer Certain Colors or Kinds of Flowers?

Butterflies are often drawn to pink, purple, and yellow flowers. But other factors also influence their choices. They are attracted by the scents of certain flowers. And the flower must have the right shape for a butterfly to reach the nectar with its proboscis.

Many butterflies like purple, pink, and yellow flowers best.

45

SOME WORDS ABOUT BUTTERFLIES AND MOTHS

camouflage: Coloring that blends in with the surroundings.

chrysalis: A butterfly pupa.

cocoon: A silken case that protects the pupae of most moths and a few butterflies.

dormant: Resting, or inactive.

exoskeleton: A hard outer shell.

habitat: The place where a plant or animal naturally lives.

hibernate: To pass the winter in a dormant state.

metamorphosis: A process through which immature animals take on a different form to become adults.

nectar: A sweet liquid found in flowers.

palpi: A moth's taste organ.

pollinate: To transfer plant pollen (male sex cells) to plant ova (female sex cells), so that plants form seeds and reproduce.

predators: Animals that catch and eat other animals.

proboscis: A tonguelike tube through which a butterfly or moth can suck nectar.

pupa (plural: **pupae**): The stage of life during which a caterpillar changes into an adult butterfly or moth. When a caterpillar enters this stage, it is said to pupate.

SOURCES FOR BUTTERFLY AND MOTH SUPPLIES

These companies sell caterpillars, cocoons, and chrysalises, as well as butterfly nets and other supplies. If you raise butterflies or moths obtained through mail-order sources such as these, be sure to release the adults only in suitable habitats.

Carolina Biological Supply
2700 York Road
Burlington, NC 27215
1-800-334-5551

Connecticut Valley Biological
82 Valley Road, P.O. Box 326
Southampton, MA 01073
1-800-628-7748

Insect Lore
P.O. Box 1535
Shafter, CA 93263
1-800-LiveBug

FOR FURTHER READING

George, Jean Craighead. *The Moon of the Monarch Butterflies.* New York: HarperCollins, 1993.

Hariton, Anca. *Butterfly Story.* New York: Dutton, 1995.

Lasky, Kathryn. *Monarchs.* San Diego: Harcourt Brace, 1993.

Lavies, Bianca. *Monarch Butterflies: Mysterious Travelers.* New York: Dutton, 1992.

Ring, Elizabeth. *Night Flier.* Brookfield, CT: Millbrook, 1994.

Taylor, Kim. *Butterfly.* New York: Dorling Kindersley, 1992.

Tesar, Jenny. *Insects.* Woodbridge, CT: Blackbirch Press, 1993.

Watts, Barrie. *Butterflies and Moths.* New York: Franklin Watts, 1991.

INDEX

Note: Page numbers in italics indicate pictures.